Corny Humor

Wit and Witticism
The Fourth Time Around

Large

Published by

the National Federation

of the Blind

Table of Contents

Introduction

I'm a true believer in the old adage that, "If you smile, the world smiles with you." And, from the tremendously favorable response to our WIT AND WITTICISM books, millions of Americans believe it too.

I started the practice of including jokes and funny stories in the National Federation of the Blind "Presidential Message" tapes back in 1968. I did this because the "Presidential Messages" were always filled with the serious problems of blindness, and I wanted to share these jokes and funny stories that had made me smile with my friends...to make them smile and take their minds off the problems of blindness for just a little while.

This fourth edition of jokes and funny stories, "CORNY HUMOR-- WIT AND WITTICISM THE FOURTH TIME AROUND" is due in large part to the many letters of thanks and encouragement we have received from people all over the country who have enjoyed reading our three other WIT AND WITTICISM books. We are pleased to present you with this all-new compilation of "Corny Humor" and funny stories.

I hope that in some small way this volume of jokes and funny stories will make you smile and lighten your day's burden...even for just a few minutes.

Kenneth Jernigan
President Emeritus

Why Large Type

The type size of this book is 14 point for two important reasons: One, because typesetting of 14 point or larger complies with federal standards for the printing of materials for visually impaired readers, and we want to show you exactly what type size is necessary for people with limited sight.

The second reason is that many of our friends and supporters have asked us to print our paperback books in 14 point type so they too can easily read them. Many people with limited sight do not use Braille. We hope that by printing this book in larger type than customary, many more people will be able to benefit from it.

Kenneth Jernigan,
President Emeritus

National Federation of the Blind

Creatures Great and Small

What do you get when you cross a rooster and a duck?

A bird that gets up at the quack of dawn.

What kind of horses go out after dark?

Night mares.

Why did Beethoven get rid of his chickens?

Because they kept saying, "Bach, Bach, Bach."

Two silk worms were in a race.

They ended up in a tie.

How do you stop a charging rhinoceros?

You take away his credit card!

What did the wicked chicken lay?

Deviled eggs.

Why did the pig want to become an actor?

He was a big ham.

What do you get when you cross the world's best fairy tale teller with the world's largest mammal?

A whale of a tale.

What's more dangerous than pulling a shark's tooth?

Giving a porcupine a back rub.

If fruit comes from a fruit tree, what kind of tree does a chicken come from?

A poul-tree!

Why do elephants have trunks?

Because they don't have pockets to put things in.

What happens when you cross a rottweiler with a collie?

You get a dog who bites off your arm and then goes to get help.

How do you find a lost rabbit?

Make a noise like a carrot.

When Chicken Little was killed on the playground his friends said it was an accident.

The police, however, suspected fowl play.

Do you know what the termite said when he walked into the bar?

"Is the bar tender here?"

Why did the elephant need a tow truck?

Because he broke his toe.

Two flies are on the porch;
which one is the actor?

The one on the screen.

What do you get when you
cross an elephant and a fish?

Swimming trunks.

Where does a penguin keep his money?

In a snow bank.

Why do male deer need braces?

Because they have buck teeth.

Some Things Never Change

A grumpy man walks into a restaurant and asks the maitre 'd: "Do you serve crabs here?"

Maitre 'd: "Why certainly, sir, have a seat."

If your motto is "If at first you don't succeed"—don't take up skydiving.

What kind of shoes do baby cowboys wear?

They wear cowboy booties.

What kinds of jokes do vegetables like best?

Corny ones!

What is the best way to carve wood?

Whittle by whittle.

Conversation heard by the coffee machine:

"Tell me, Sam, how long have you been working here?"

"Ever since they threatened to fire me!"

17

Why did the city slicker
hunters quit hunting elephants?

Because they got tired of
carrying the decoys.

What did the bedspread say
to the sheet?

I've got you covered.

A rooster lays an egg on the peak of a roof. Which side of the roof does the egg roll down?

Neither, because roosters don't lay eggs.

What stays in bed most of the day and sometimes goes to the bank?

A stream.

Why does a milking stool only have three legs?

Because the cow has the udder.

What did the finger say to the thumb?

I'm in glove with you.

Why are people who live on a hill never trustworthy?

Because they're not on the level.

How can you tell that a right angle has been to school?

It has 90 degrees.

Funny But Real Headlines

Police Begin Campaign to Run Down Jaywalkers

Eye Drops Off Shelf

Teacher Strikes Idle Kids

Squad Helps Dog
Bite Victim

Enraged Cow Injures
Farmer With Ax

Drunken Drivers
Paid $1000

Juvenile Court to Try Shooting Defendant

Stolen Painting Found by Tree

A Commentary on Culture

Father: How were your test scores, Son?

Son: Underwater, Dad.

Father: What do you mean underwater?

Son: You know, below C level.

Once I got angry at the chef at an Italian restaurant, so I gave him a pizza my mind.

Why did the book join the police?

So he could work undercover.

Why do florescent lights always hum?

Because they don't know the words.

Why do we dress baby boys in blue and baby girls in pink?

Because they can't dress themselves.

Why did the man run around his bed?

Because he wanted to catch up on his sleep.

Why are movie stars cool?

Because they have so many fans.

A man walked into a lawyer's office and inquired about the lawyer's rates.

"$50 for three questions", replied the lawyer.

"Isn't that awfully steep?" asked the man.

"Yes," the lawyer said, "and what was your third question?"

How many hired hands does it take to change a light bulb?

It takes lots of them. For we all know, "Many hands make light work."

Everyone has a photographic memory.

Some just don't have film.

Riddles Galore

Where do tough chickens come from?

Hard boiled eggs.

Why did the house go to the doctor?

To get a cure for its window pane.

What did Elsie the cow pack in her suitcase when she went on vacation?

Her Moo Moo.

What is round and really violent?

A vicious circle.

Why would Snow White be a good judge?

Because she's the fairest in the land.

What did the ant do when he killed the other ant?

He committed pesticide.

What did the lawyer name
her daughter?

Sue.

What did the cook name his
son?

Stu.

What did the hamburger
name her daughter?

Patty.

What did the mountain
climber name his son?

Cliff.

A Judicial Sense of Humor

Actual Questions Asked in Court Rooms

"How many times have you committed suicide?"

"Were you alone or by yourself?"

"How far apart were the cars when the collision occurred?"

"Now doctor, isn't it true that when a person dies in his sleep, he doesn't know about it until the next morning?"

"Were you present when your picture was taken?"

"You were there until the time you left, is that true?"

"These stairs that went down to the basement, did they go up, also?"

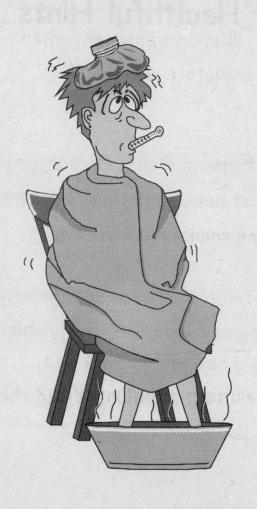

Healthful Hints

Patient: Please Doctor, you must help me, I think I'm losing my memory.

Doctor: Is that so! For how long have you had this problem?

Patient: What problem?

A man ran into a doctor's office and said, "Doctor, Doctor, you've got to help me. I feel like a deck of cards!"

The doctor replied, "Please sit down and I'll deal with you later."

Another man ran into the same doctor yelling, "Doctor, Doctor, I feel like a pair of curtains!"

"Come on," said the doctor, "pull yourself together."

A French poodle and a collie were walking down the street. The poodle complained to the collie, "My life is a mess; my owner is mean; my mate is having an affair with a German shepherd and I'm as nervous as a cat."

"Why don't you go see a psychiatrist?" asked the collie.

"I can't," replied the poodle, "I'm not allowed on the couch."

How many psychologists does it take to change a light bulb?

Just one, but the light bulb really has to want to change.

Why do doctors have to keep their tempers?

Because they don't want to lose their patients.

For Your Information

What do you get when you cross a sheep and a bee?

A Bahumbug.

How could anybody be a masochist?

Beats me.

When your pet bird sees you reading the newspaper, does he wonder why you're just sitting there, staring at the carpeting?

Where can you enjoy fascinating characters at breakfast?

In a cereal novel.

Despite the cost of living, have you noticed how it remains so popular?

Why does a bike stand on one leg?

Because it's two-tired.

Why can't you send a telegram to Washington?

Because he's dead.

Do they have a 4th of July in England?

Yes. (They also have a 3rd of July, a 2nd of July, etc.)

How many birthdays does the average man have?

One a year.

Some months have 31 days. How many have 28?

All of them.

Why can't a man living in the USA be buried in Canada?

Because he's still alive.

Why shouldn't you wear snow boots?

Because they'll melt.

Publicity: The art of putting the best feat forward.

Antique: Something no one would be seen with if there were more of them, but which everyone wants when no one else has any.

Ex-king: One who has come in out of the reign.

One way to save face is to keep the lower half of it shut.

What kind of clothing does a house wear?

Address.

What runs around the cow pasture but never moves?

The fence.

Where can you find an ocean without water?

On a map.

What kind of bugs do knights fight?

Dragonflies.

How do you fix a broken tomato?

With tomato paste.

Culture Shock

Why do people in Ireland take their money to the bank?

Because it's always Dublin.

What do sea monsters have for dinner?

Fish and ships.

Two boll weevils grew up in South Carolina. One went to Hollywood and became a famous actor.

The other stayed behind in the cotton fields and never amounted to much.

The second one, naturally, was the lesser of two weevils.

When high school kids
wear rags today,

they call it self-expression.

When I was young
and dressed that way,

we called it the Depression.

Why did they find bones on the moon?

The cow never made it.

What do people from Minneapolis call a small cola?

A mini-soda.

Why did the cucumber
blush?

He saw the salad dressing.

What did one magnet say to
the other?

I find you very attractive.

Life in the Fast Lane

Why did the coach flood the gym?

Because he wanted to send in a sub.

How does a man on the moon get his hair cut?

Eclipse it.

Why did the boy stick a hose in his friend's ear?

Because he wanted to brainwash him.

Bob: Do you like raisin bread?

Jim: Don't know, never raised any.

Who are the longest
speakers?

Prisoners--they can spend a
lifetime on a single sentence.

Why did the coach send in
his second string?

He wanted to tie up the game.

What did the alien say to the gas pump?

Take your fingers out of your ears and listen to me!

What did one campfire say to the other?

Let's go out one of these days.

Why do cowboys roll the sides of their Stetsons?

So they can get three in a pickup.

A Special Kind of Wisdom

Why does Santa like to work on his garden on his day off?

So he can hoe, hoe, hoe.

If two is a couple and three is a crowd, what is four and five?

Nine

Change is inevitable, except from a vending machine.

I wonder how much deeper the ocean would be without sponges.

Which animal keeps the best time?

A watch dog.

Did you hear about the skeleton who went to the library to "bone-up"?

What does a houseboat become when it grows up?

A township.

What happened when the wheel was invented?

There was a revolution.

What three letters turn a girl into a woman?

A-G-E.

What has no beginning, no end, and nothing in the middle?

A doughnut.

Why did the man put his car in the oven?

Because he wanted a hot rod.

What can you wear anytime that never goes out of style?

A smile.

Why do baby pigs eat so much?

They want to make hogs of themselves.

Where do cows go on a
Saturday night?

To the mooooo-vies.

On which side does a
leopard have the most spots?

On the outside!

Ghostly Humor

Where should you send mail
to a ghost?

To the "dead letter"
department.

Who wrote the recent best-
seller about haunted houses?

A ghostwriter, of course.

Why aren't ghosts very popular at parties?

Because they aren't much to look at!

Where do you find a missing ghost?

At his favorite haunt.

An older brother was trying to scare his little brother so he asked him to imagine that they were trapped alone in a haunted house full of ghosts.

When he asked him what he would do, the little boy calmly replied:

"I'll just stop imagining!"

What is a witch's favorite subject?

Spelling.

Where do goblins go swimming?

Lake Eerie.

What does a ghost call his mother and father?

Trans-parents.

How do you make a witch itch?

Take away her "w".

Help Change What It Means To Be Blind By Taking These Actions

☑ Take time to learn what blind people are really like. Get to know one of us on a personal basis.

☑ Promote Braille literacy. Insist that blind children be taught Braille in the public schools. Blind children who can't read can't compete.

☑ Tell an employer that blind people can be good employees. Blind people face a 70% unemployment rate. You can help.

☑ Seek out parents of blind children. Help form a support group in your community. Informed parents give children opportunities.

☑ Distribute Kernel Books (stories about the capabilities of blind persons) to local public libraries and schools.

☑ Tell others the things you know about the capabilities of blind people and the help available to them-- friends, family members, employers, and community leaders. Understanding what blindness really means is the true key to solving the problems blind people face.

NATIONAL FEDERATION OF THE BLIND

We Care About You Too! If a friend or family member needs assistance with problems of blindness, please write: Marc Maurer, President, 1800 Johnson Street, Suite 300, Baltimore, Maryland 21230-4998.